Lil' Romeo!

by Michael-Anne Johns

W9-BNK-854

SCHOLASTIC INC.

New York · Toronto · London · Auckland · Sydney · Mexico City · New Delhi · Hong Kong · Buenos Aires

Photo Credits

Front cover: Ernie Paniccioli/Retna, Ltd.; Back cover: John Ricard/Retna Ltd.; Page 1: Kwaku Alston/Corbis Outline; Page 2: Jeff Kravitz/FilmMagic.com; Page 3: (top) Mike Guastella/WireImage.com; Page 3: (bottom) Mike Guastella/WireImage.com; Page 4: Guastella/WireImage.com; Page 5: Steve Grayson/WireImage.com; Page 6: John Ricard/ Retna Ltd.; Page 7: Michael Caulfield/WireImage.com; Page 8: John Ricard/Retna Ltd.

This book is UNAUTHORIZED and not affiliated with Lil' Romeo or any of his representatives.

If you purchased this book without a cover, you should be aware that this book is stolen property. It was reported as "unsold and destroyed" to the publisher, and neither the author nor the publisher has received any payment for this "stripped book."

No part of this publication may be reproduced in whole or part, or stored in a retrieval system, or transmitted in any form or by any means, electronic, mechanical, photocopying, recording, or otherwise, without written permission of the publisher. For information regarding permission, write to Scholastic Inc., Attention: Permissions Department, 555 Broadway, New York, NY 10012.

ISBN: 0-439-63621-3

Copyright © 2004 Scholastic Inc.
All rights reserved. Published by Scholastic Inc.
SCHOLASTIC and associated logos are trademarks and/or registered trademarks of Scholastic Inc.

Designed by Bethany Dixon
Photo Editor: Sharon Lennon

12 11 10 9 8 7 6 5 4 3 2 1   4 5 6 7 8 9/0

Printed in the U.S.A.
First printing, February 2004

CONTENTS PAGE

INTRODUCTION

Are you Lil' Romeo's number one fan?
Do you know the lyrics to all his songs?
Have you written him and shared your
  feelings with him?

Well, if you can answer a resounding YES to
the questions above, this *Pop People* is the book for
YOU! It's got all the hot and cool stuff Lil' Romeo
fans want to know about — from the down-lo to the
shout-it-in-the-streets info. It's all here!

Lil' Romeo is more than a cartoon-loving, hoop-
shooting, beat-rapping teen. When he was only
eleven years old, Lil' Romeo took his lead from his
superstar rapper dad, Master P, and released his
first self-titled album. The album's first single, "My
Baby," zoomed *up* the record charts — and flew *out*

1

of the record stores. He followed *Lil' Romeo* with another chart-topping album, *Game Time*, and toured the country. He also guested on TV shows like *Soul Train* and Nickelodeon's *The Nick Cannon Show*, and appeared in the movie *Max Keeble's Big Move*.

The year 2003 was a biggie for this lil' shorty. Lil' Romeo hooked up with the Nickelodeon network and debuted in his own TV series, *Romeo!*. And just two months later, he joined actress Jessica Alba in a starring role in the film *Honey*.

For you true-blue Lil' Romeo fans, this is just the beginning — there's going to be lots more music, movies, and fun from this multitalented teenager. So sit back and flip through the following pages for Lil' Romeo's life story, fun facts, and even some super secrets!

CHAPTER 1
All in the Family

Rap and music have been the soundtrack of Lil' Romeo's entire life. From the day he was born — August 19, 1989 — Percy Romeo Miller III has listened to the hip-hop beat. It's in his bones, his heart, and his soul.

Of course, that's true of a lot of city kids, but not all of them have Percy Romeo Miller II — otherwise known as Master P — as their father. Today, Master P is a multiplatinum artist and CEO of one of the most successful independent record labels, New No Limit Records. But when Lil' Romeo was born to Percy and Sonja Miller the bling-bling lifestyle wasn't part of the scene for them. As a matter of fact, the family lived in a New Orleans housing project. Money was short back then, but Percy had big dreams.

Percy's two loves were basketball and rap, and

3

he spent much of his own childhood on the basketball court and practicing his rap skills. Percy and his brothers lived with their grandparents, Big Mama and Big Daddy Miller. He credits them with giving the family love, roots, and stability. Master P says Big Mama "raised us to be what we are now." And that self-reliance and determination was something he wanted to pass on to his own kids.

"I had to struggle young — I mean, I grew up in the ghetto," recalls Master P. "Romeo has an opportunity to see life from another angle, like, when he was growing up in the ghetto, he was very little. My whole struggle was to take us out of there. Now he's getting a chance to see life from another side. We are financially wealthy now, but we still understand the values that we come from. For us life was a struggle. We couldn't go to the best schools, we couldn't have a tutor. You gotta take the past and build from that, make a better way out for you and your family."

The First Step

Around the time Lil' Romeo was born, Percy had decided to concentrate on starting his own independent hip-hop record label. With a small inheritance

4

from his grandfather, Percy laid the foundation of what would eventually become No Limit Records — later redubbed New No Limit Records.

Percy took on the professional name Master P and went to work in the studio. He wrote, produced, and made albums, and before he even had a company office, Master P sold over 500,000 albums out of the back of his car. "Gold from my trunk," laughs the mega-mogul now.

All the while Master P and his brothers were throwing down rhymes, Lil' Romeo was listening — and learning. When he was only four years old, Lil' Romeo was watching his dad and uncles perform, and occasionally he joined them on stage.

"I used to watch [my dad] a lot a long time ago, like when I was five years old," says Lil' Romeo. "I used to talk on [his] intros. I could barely talk. It was fun."

Master P liked having his son with him in the studio and on stage, but he didn't take it too seriously. At the time, Master P had no idea his son had major rhyming skills.

Neither did Lil' Romeo's uncle, rapper Silkk the Shocker. "I remember he was like, 'Silkk, put me on track, let me rap on this beat,'" the rapper says of Lil' Romeo. "I told him, 'Boy, stop playing.' He was seven or eight. But he was writing his own lyrics and he and some of his friends got some karaoke equipment and started rapping over a beat. I was like, 'That don't sound bad, it's aiight.'"

Once Lil' Romeo had his uncle in his corner, he made his move. "I used to see my dad and all his brothers rhyming, so I knew I wanted to do it one day," Lil' Romeo explains. "Me and my cousin used to sneak in his studio and make songs. The producer was mixing a song one day that I had recorded a rap on while my dad was out on tour."

When Master P got home, he heard the rap. "My dad was like, 'Who's that?' and the producer was like, 'That's Romeo,'" recalls Romeo. "That's how it got started."

"I found it amazing just to come home and find out that he has the talent he has," Master P says. "He would always play around and rap with his cousins. But this is something that he never had to do, so to hear what he wrote — I just thought it was incredible."

In The Studio

Romeo and his dad sat down and really had a heart-to-heart. Master P was willing to give his son all the props to start putting together a demo tape, but he wanted Lil' Romeo to know about the downside of the business, too. There were going to be a lot of things that Lil' Romeo would have to sacrifice if he wanted to pursue a career in the music business, Master P explained. He would have to work really hard, and that would mean giving up a lot of hanging out and playtime with his friends and family. And, most important, Lil' Romeo would have to keep his grades up no matter what. Education came first, before music, basketball, and everything else!

Master P put Lil' Romeo in the studio with some super producers from the No Limit family — Diesel of Soulja Music Production and C-Los Beats. "They [made some] songs," remembers Master P. "I asked to hear one of 'em and was like, 'Oh yeah, this kid is ready.'"

The result was eleven-year-old Lil' Romeo's debut album — *Lil' Romeo*. "My Baby," the first single, set the tone for the whole Lil' Romeo project. It blew up the charts! As a matter of fact, "My Baby" went to the top of the pop and rap and R&B charts. It stayed in the number one position for ten weeks, which made Lil' Romeo the youngest artist to have a number one song on the charts. Not only was it exciting, but the artist Lil' Romeo took that particular honor from was one of his all-time idols, Michael Jackson, who had also been eleven years old when his single "Ben" topped the charts. According to *Billboard* magazine, "Lil' Romeo is the youngest artist to ever reach number one on a solo project and also the youngest rap artist to achieve that status."

Full Circle

The success of *Lil' Romeo* didn't go to the young rapper's head. He was determined not to be a one-hit wonder, either. So, after dropping two more singles from *Lil' Romeo*, he went right back into the studio to work on his second album, *Game Time*. And, while keeping his grades in the all-A's-and-B's level, Lil' Romeo juggled school, playing basketball for the American Athletic Union Junior League, and making his big-screen debut in the film *Max Keeble's Big Move*. And during break time, Lil' Romeo worked with his dad on some movie scripts and TV series ideas. The result? In September 2003, he and his dad, Master P, debuted in their own Nickelodeon TV series, *Romeo!* And in November 2003, Lil' Romeo starred in the movie *Honey* with TV's *Dark Angel* star, Jessica Alba.

With all the success Lil' Romeo has had, he also

feels it is important to share. That's a lesson he's learned from his parents. Although most of the time the Millers reach out and help others without much fanfare, they did allow the CBS TV crew from *48 Hours Investigates* to accompany them on a trip back to their old neighborhood. It was a far cry from the luxurious homes and life they now have. But they weren't there to front. No — they wanted to share a message: Hard work pays off, and when you succeed, give back.

During the *48 Hours* segment, Master P and Lil' Romeo stopped by St. Monica's Elementary School, where they were greeted with cheers, but not just because they are platinum-selling artists. St. Monica's was on the verge of closing because they couldn't meet their budget. When Master P heard his old elementary school was about to close its doors, he stepped up to the plate and provided enough funds for them to stay open and continue to give the kids of the neighborhood a good education.

"We always tell the [kids], always get your education, because if you have your education, you can accomplish anything," explained Lil' Romeo to the TV reporter. "You know, stay humble. Don't change for nobody."

CHAPTER 2
Superstar Time Line

An at-a-glance look at the highlights of Lil' Romeo's life!

August 19, 1989	Percy Romeo Miller Jr. was born in New Orleans, Louisiana.
May 1, 2001	*Lil' Romeo* was released in the UK.
May 23, 2001	Lil' Romeo released his very first single, "My Baby."
July 3, 2001	*Lil' Romeo,* his debut album, was released in the United States.
July 8, 2001	Lil' Romeo TEENick Concert aired.
August 7, 2001	"My Baby" was released in the UK.
March 8, 2002	Lil' Romeo started the Lil'

	Romeo 2002 Tour in Jacksonville, Florida.
December 17, 2002	Lil' Romeo released his second album, *Game Time*.
January 21, 2003	P. Miller Shorties clothing line is introduced exclusively to Mervyn stores all over the country.
June 11, 2003	Lil' Romeo and Master P are featured on the CBS news program *48 Hours Investigates*. It focused on showbiz's richest kids, such as *Malcolm in the Middle*'s Frankie Muniz and Mary Kate and Ashley Olsen.
September 13, 2003	*Romeo!,* Lil' Romeo's first TV series, debuted on Nickelodeon.
November 14, 2003	*Honey*, Lil' Romeo's feature film with Jessica Alba, hit the movie theaters.

Now It's Your Turn!

Put on your thinking cap and make a time line of your own life. List all the important dates and de-

11

tails that you remember. Show it to your parents and maybe they'll remember a few moments you forgot. We'll start you off with some suggestions.

My Birthday: _____

My First Step: _____

My First Word: _____

My Younger Brother's/Sister's Birthday: _____

_____

My First Day at School: _____

_____

My First Bike: _____

My First Vacation: _____

Keep going!

_____

_____

_____

_____

_____

_____

_____

_____

_____

_____

_____

CHAPTER 3

Lil' Romeo Talk Soup

X-clusive Q & A . . . Just 4 U

Check out this private one-on-one Q & A session with Lil' Romeo. He answers questions about his family, friends, and favorite sports, video games, and all his many adventures. Read on!

Q: Do you remember something really cool that happened when you were very young?
Lil' Romeo: I'll just say when I first got my first Big Wheel car. I used to drive it up and down the little sidewalks with my cousins and my brothers, and race it, and that was a lot of fun.

Q: When you started out at age eleven, you were one of the youngest people in the hip-

hop music scene. Do you feel like you're treated like an adult or like a kid?

Lil' Romeo: I'm trying to stay like a regular kid because I'm a regular person, so I still try to do regular things. People still treat me as a kid because I don't want to rush my life.

Q: You've grown up in the spotlight. Do you ever feel like it's hard being famous?

Lil' Romeo: I was always with my dad [even before I started to perform], so I saw a little bit of what it was going to be like. But me, I'm having a lot of fun with it. I still try to do regular things, like play on my basketball team, go to school, and go to the mall.

Q: Are you still going to regular classes or are you being tutored?

Lil' Romeo: I go to a private school and then when I'm on the road I have a tutor. Education always comes first, because when I won't be doing this, I want to have an education.

Q: You have told a lot of people that math is your favorite subject — why do you like it so much?

Lil' Romeo: It's the most challenging subject to me and it's just a lot of fun. Oh yeah, that's one of my favorite things, solving problems. If it weren't for math I probably wouldn't want to go to school as much.

Q: It's great that you're out there telling kids how important it is to get a good education. Do you sing about that theme in your music?
Lil' Romeo: Education always comes first. Always listen to your parents. [I] teach them that in the songs. I always give them something to believe in and [tell them to] have a lot of fun in [their] life.

Q: Where did you learn the importance of education?
Lil' Romeo: My mom and my dad were the ones who taught me what education really means. If I don't get A's and B's, there's no music or touring.

Q: One of the things that you've talked about is the importance of doing normal kid things. With all of the entertainment stuff you're involved in, how do you find time to do everyday, normal things?
Lil' Romeo: My dad keeps me grounded, because you have to be grounded to be successful. I just believe in staying regular, even if I become the biggest star.

15

Q: When did you know that you wanted to be a solo rapper?

Lil' Romeo: My cousins and I used to rap a lot by ourselves, and make our own songs on a karaoke machine. One day, my dad asked me if I wanted to perform, and I said yes. That's how I got started.

Q: Describe what your stage show is like.

Lil' Romeo: Usually we have one or two large TV screens behind me so you could see the video to whatever song I'm performing. At the beginning we have a cartoon with Bugs Bunny, then my cousin dances with the dancers. Then I come out of the smoke and we start performing.

Q: What does it feel like to have all of those fans screaming for you?

Lil' Romeo: It's a little bit scary, but I'm used to it and I know that they really like what I'm doing. It feels real good to know that they're there.

Q: You opened for 'N Sync on their tour when you were only eleven years old. Was that fun?

Lil' Romeo: It was real fun. My mom came with me. I like to see all the fans out there. This was one of the first times I traveled. I never thought there was so much traveling in the music business, but it's fun. If I [weren't] having fun, I wouldn't be doing this. 'N Sync are very nice. I hung out with Justin [Timberlake] a lot.

Q: Did you teach him how to rap?
Lil' Romeo: Nah, not yet!

Q: How did you feel when you found out that "My Baby," your first single from your debut CD, *Romeo*, broke Michael Jackson's record?
Lil' Romeo: I felt very good. I used to admire him a lot. I like a lot of his songs, like, "ABC."

Q: Tell us about your CD *Game Time*.
Lil' Romeo: It's a real positive album, up-tempo songs and slow songs, so it's a lot of fun. I always write a lot of my songs because [otherwise] it won't be me. My dad will go over it to see if I need to change any things. . . . I made it for everyone to listen to — grown ups, teenagers, and kids.

Q: What is your writing process like?
Lil' Romeo: I usually do the hook first, so I know

what to sing about. I just like to write about what kids like to hear. I ask myself, "If I was a kid, what would I like to hear?"

Q: Do you have any special places you like to write, or do you just jot things down when they come to you?
Lil' Romeo: When I'm on an airplane, me and my dad just come up with stuff. Like, he'll have a dream and be like, "I came up with an idea." And then we'll write on the plane.

Q: What is it like to write songs with your dad?
Lil' Romeo: It's a lot of fun! You know you're going to have a hit song when he's with you. He tells me my dos and don'ts, so writing is a lot of fun.

Q: When you decide you're going to write a song, how do you do it? Do you think of a lyric or a theme?
Lil' Romeo: When I write, I first listen to the beat, then I think about what kind of song I should put on this beat. I think if I want to make an up-tempo song, and what I want it to be about. My audience is a lot of kids so I make real positive kids' music.

Q: Is the house featured on MTV's *Cribs* your house or one of your parents' houses?

Lil' Romeo: That's my house. It's a future investment because I'm a kid, so I still live with my mom and my dad, but I'm just thinking for the future.

Q: What are some of your favorite things in your houses?

Lil' Romeo: We have a lot of scooter bikes and mopeds. We always have a basketball court at all the houses because I love to play basketball.

Q: What room do you spend most of your time in when you are home?

Lil' Romeo: The studio, we're in there 24/7. I sleep in there sometimes. And probably the game room a lot, because everybody studies in the game room. It's one of the biggest rooms.

Q: In 2001 you were named the top player in The American Amateur Games. What is that?

Lil' Romeo: It's a junior Olympic league for kids. You have to win in your state, and the best three teams from the state get to go to one city and play against all the best teams from around the world. We got second in the nation last year.

Q: Where is your team based?
Lil' Romeo: Our team is from Houston, Texas — they are called the No Limit Ballers. I'm a point guard.

Q: What moves are you known for?
Lil' Romeo: Crossovers, and I can dribble real well, shoot 3's. While I'm in the air I put the ball under my leg and do a layup with it.

Q: Your dad, Master P, actually played with some NBA teams — did you get your love and knowledge of basketball from him?
Lil' Romeo: I used to watch my dad a lot while he was playing. I used to watch the NBA. My favorite players are Kobe Bryant and Allen Iverson, so I watch them and get moves from them. They are my two favorite players, but I know Shaq. I know him because he lived in Louisiana and he used to live right next to us.

Q: What's your dad's best move on the court?
Lil' Romeo: A little shake 'n' bake crossover thing, then he shoots a long, long three.

Q: What's your favorite thing to do: play basketball or write and perform music?
Lil' Romeo: Right now I'm focusing on my music, but in the future I'm going to be a NBA player.

Q: If you weren't performing on stage, what do you think you would choose as a career?
Lil' Romeo: I like to study stars, astronomy stuff. And like I said — I'm going to be a NBA player. And own a business!

Q: What has been the most difficult thing so far for you in your career or in your life?
Lil' Romeo: In my career, it's [been hard] being away from my family a lot. That's the only thing. You have to go on the road and tour. I'm usually with my family, but I was alone for, like, two weeks before — that's probably the longest. Usually they'll come out on the road with me or I'll hurry up and go home.

Q: What is it like when you are on the road touring?
Lil' Romeo: When I go on tour, I have a big 'ol bus that we travel in. It's just a lot of fun — that's what came in the package to be a pop star/rap star.

Q: Is there anything about being famous that's hard for you — like seeing your picture everywhere or being followed by fans?

Lil' Romeo: Well, that is something that comes in the package, too. You know somebody is always going to want an autograph or something, so you just got to get ready for it.

Q: Does it make you nervous when you hear girls screaming and they start chasing you?

Lil' Romeo: When I wasn't Lil' Romeo and I used to be at my school, everybody was still doing that because my dad is Master P and I used to go on the road with him. Everybody said, "Who is that?" It's a little bit scary, but I'm used to it and know that they really are thankful for me and like what I'm doing. I just feel real good to know that they're there.

Q: You made your big screen debut in the film *Max Keeble's Big Move*. Did you have fun when you were filming it?

Lil' Romeo: We had a lot of fun. We were in the burger shop and we had to drink a whole bunch of milk shakes because we had to film takes over and over, but it was very fun.

Q: In September 2003 you began your first TV series, *Romeo!*, on Nickelodeon. What's it all about?

Lil' Romeo: It's like a modern day *Partridge Family* type of thing. It's a lot of fun and it [deals with] some of the kid issues and things about school, like peer pressure and just being with your family. My dad is going to be on it.

Q: Rapping, touring, getting good grades, playing basketball . . . that's a lot for one person to deal with. How do you manage it all?

Lil' Romeo: I just focus on what I'm doing at the time. When I'm at school, I focus on school. I don't have a schedule for everything. When I'm done with school, I go home, lay down, play basketball, practice rapping, and do my homework. I focus on whatever I'm doing, so I can always do it better.

Q: Have you gotten used to all of the attention you receive from fans, or are you still a little shy?

Lil' Romeo: I'm not shy when I perform. The only thing I [worry] about is tripping on stage.

Q: You've traveled all over the world. Do you have a favorite place that you would like to visit again?

Lil' Romeo: Hawaii, my favorite place. I went there [when I was about six or seven]. That's when I first went [there], and I still remember everything that I did. I bought shoes there that weren't out here yet — FILA shoes. I went home bragging about them and nobody else had them but me and my mom. We went in a submarine and things. We only went for a little while because my sister was too young, so we were only able to go for a little bit. And in the hotel there was a big ol' slide that came from one of the doors or something on the third floor and it took, like, two minutes to get down, and that was a lot of fun. So, I had a great time in Hawaii.

Q: Sometimes people try to make a competition between you and Bow Wow. Aren't you two really friends?

Lil' Romeo: Yeah. We first met in Atlanta when he first started rapping. We might do a song together, but it's not a competition thing between him and me. That's the way I feel about it.

CHAPTER 4

Lil' of This . . . Lil' of That

Check out the ultimate Lil' Romeo stax-o-fax!

THE BASICS
Full Name: Percy Romeo Miller III
Stage Name: Lil' Romeo
Nickname: Rome or Romie
Secret Nickname: "I tell [people] to call me Leo. That's my secret name. Leo's my birth sign, and the lion's my favorite animal."
Birthday: August 19, 1989
Astrological Sun Sign: Leo
Birthplace: New Orleans, Louisiana
Current Residences: Baton Rouge, Louisiana, Houston, Texas, and Los Angeles, California
Parents: Dad, Master P; mom, Sonja

Siblings: Two brother, three sisters — all younger
Pets: A white terrier named Dollar; a parakeet named Purty
Hometown School: St. Luke's Episcopal School in Baton Rouge, Louisiana — when Romeo is working in the studio or on the road, he studies with a tutor.
Cars: A mini Mercedes Benz and a mini Hummer — even though he's not old enough to drive! The mini Benz even has a fake license plate that reads "LiRomeo"
Basketball Team: No Limit Ballers
Albums: *Lil' Romeo* and *Game Time*
First Single: "My Baby"
First TV Series: Nickelodeon's *Romeo!*
First TV Special: *Teen Nick* concert series
Movies: *Max Keeble's Big Move, Honey, Uncle P*
Self-Description: "Outgoing, fun-loving, and energetic."

FUN FAVES
Fave Body Parts: His arms and stomach
Fave School Subjects: Math and English
Fave Music: R&B, pop, rock
Fave Pop Singers: Britney Spears and 'N Sync

Fave Hip-Hoppers: His dad, Master P; his uncle, Silkk; Bow Wow, and Nelly

Fave Female Rapper: Eve

Fave Male R&B Singer: Usher

Fave Female R&B Singers: Mya, Solange, and Alicia Keys

Fave Book: *Johnny Long Legs* by Matt Christopher

Fave Indoor Sport: Basketball — he plays point guard

Fave Basketball Move: The crossover

Fave NBA Team: L.A. Lakers

Fave NBA Players: Philadelphia '76er Allen Iverson and L.A. Lakers Kobe Bryant and Shaquille O'Neal

All Time Fave NBA Player: Michael Jordan

Fave Outdoor Team Sports: Football and soccer

Fave Water Sport: Jet-skiing

Fave Cars: Lamborghini, Mercedes Benz, and Ferrari

Least Fave Sport: Golf

Least Fave Activity: Yoga

Fave Stores: The Gap and Mervyns

Fave Food: Pizza

Fave Snack at Home: Macaroni and cheese

Fave Fast-Food Restaurant: McDonald's

Fave Fast-Food Meal: McDonald's Egg, Cheese and Bacon Biscuits

Fave Ice Cream: Pralines and Cream and Butter-Rum

Fave Colors: All shades of red and blue

Fave Animal: Lion — "I'm a Leo!"

Fave Pastime: Watching cartoons and playing video games

Fave Video Platforms: Dreamcast, PlayStation2, GameCube

Fave Video Games: NBA 2K1, NFL 2K1, NBA Courtside, and James Bond

Fave Movie: *The Lion King*

Fave Musical Movie: *Grease*

Fave TV Series: *Fresh Prince of Bel Air*

Fave Old-Time Cartoon: *Bugs Bunny*

Fave Current Cartoon: *SpongeBob Squarepants*

Fave Songs of His: "Little Star" from *Lil' Romeo* — "I helped write it about my mom, 'cause she is the greatest mom I could have." "We Can Make It Right" from *Game Time*

Fave Vacation Place: Hawaii

Best Christmas Gift Received: An iPod he got for Christmas 2002

Most Prized Possession: Stevie Wonder's keyboard

Now It's Your Turn!

You've just checked out Lil' Romeo's up-close-and-personal facts and faves. Maybe you even share some of Lil' Romeo's likes and dislikes! Are you a *SpongeBob Squarepants* fan? Is the new Britney Spears or Mya CD in your backpack? Take a minute and fill out your own stax-o-fax sheet to see how much you have in common with the romantic rapper!

THE BASICS

Full Name: _____

Nickname:_____

Birthday:_____

Astrological Sun Sign: _____

Birthplace: _____

Current Residence:_____

Parents: _____

Siblings:_____

Pets: _____

School: _____

Self-Description: _____

FUN FAVES

Fave Body Parts: whole body

Fave School Subjects: art, math

Fave Music: Rap, R and B, pop

Fave Pop Singers: Britney spears

Fave Hip-Hoppers: Bow wow, Nelly, Romeo

Fave Female Rapper: The girl who sings Milkshake

Fave Female R&B Singers: Alicia keys

Fave Male R&B Singer: Usher

Fave Book: Lil' Romeo by Nicael-Ann John

Fave Sport: BasketBall

Fave Sports Team: 76sixer, LA Lakers

Fave Pro Sports Players: Allen Iverson

Fave Cars:

Least Fave Sport: Golf

Least Fave Activity: Yoga

Fave Stores: Walmart

Fave Food: pizza

Fave Snack at Home: chips, pudding

Fave Fast-Food Restaurant: Mcdonalds

Fave Fast-Food Meal: fries, nuggets

Fave Ice Cream: choclate

Fave Colors: Blue

Fave Animal: Monkey

Fave Pastime: Watching Disney Channel

Fave Video Platforms: Game Cube

Fave Video Games: _NBA on NBC_

Fave Movie: _Angre Managment_

Fave Musical Movie: _____

Fave TV Series: _Fresh prince of Bel air_

Fave Old-Time Cartoon: _Bugs Bunny_

Fave Current Cartoon: _Sponge Bob Square Pants_

Fave Vacation Place: _Puerto Rico_

Best Christmas Gift Received: _DVD player_

Most Prized Possession: _DVD player and_
play statsion

CHAPTER 5

Lil's Lists

Chart Toppers
"My Baby"
* *Billboard*'s #1 Hot Rap Single
* *Billboard*'s #1 Hot R&B/Hip-Hop Single Sales
* *Billboard*'s #1 Hot 100 Single Sales

Awards
* Rap Artist of the Year for "My Baby" — 2001 *Billboard* Music Awards
* Rap Single of the Year for "My Baby" — 2001 *Billboard* Music Awards
* 2002 *Billboard* R&B/Hip-Hop Singles Sales Award for "My Baby"
* Nickelodeon's Kids Choice Award — 2002

Honors
* Lil' Romeo is the youngest solo artist to have a

number one single — "My Baby" stayed at the top spot for 10 weeks. He actually broke Michael Jackson's record for "Ben."

* Lil' Romeo was on the Junior Olympics basketball team.
* Lil' Romeo and Master P were the cover subjects of the April 2002 issue of *The Source.*
* Master P, his wife Sonja, and their six children were the first hip-hop family to be on the cover of *Ebony* magazine.

Discography

* *Lil' Romeo* Singles
  1. Intro
  2. "Little Star"
  3. "My Baby"
  4. "The Girlies"
  5. "That's Kool" (remix)
  6. "Somebody's in Love"
  7. "Make You Dance"
  8. "My First" (remix)
  9. "I Want To Be Like You"
  10. "Little Souljas Need Love, Too"
  11. "Your ABC's"
  12. "When I Get Grown"
  13. "Remember"

14. "Where They At"
15. "Game"
16. "Don't Want To"
17. "What"
18. "Take My Pain Away"

* *Game Time Singles*
1. Intro
2. "Too Long"
3. "Play Like Us"
4. "True Love"
5. "Clap Your Hands"
6. "Girlfriend and Boyfriend"
7. "Bring It"
8. "Wanna Grow Up"
9. "Still Be There"
10. "Commercial"
11. "Feel Like Dancing"
12. "Richie Rich"
13. "My Biz"
14. "Throw Em Up"
15. "We in There"
16. "Where They At 2"
17. "Make You Dance"
18. "2 Way"
19. "We Can Make It Right"

20. "Behind the Scenes Footage" [DVD]
21. "Getting to Know Lil' Romeo" [DVD]
22. "True Love" [DVD]
23. "2 Way" [DVD]

* Theme Songs and Soundtracks
1. *Static Shock* (TV series — season 3) (rapper: theme song)
2. "Parents Just Don't Understand" with Nick Cannon and 3LW for the movie *Jimmy Neutron: Boy Genius* soundtrack
3. *Romeo!* (Nickelodeon TV series)
4. Nickelodeon network theme song: "First Kids Network"

Filmography
1. *Max Keeble's Big Move* (2001) — plays himself
2. *Honey* (2003) — Benny
3. *Uncle P* (upcoming)
4. *Shorty* (upcoming)

TV-ology
1. *The Making of* Jimmy Neutron (2001)
2. *Oh Drama!* (Musical Guest) (November 1, 2001)
3. *The Hughleys* (played himself in episode: "Daddy's Lil' Girl") (November 5, 2001)
4. *MTV's Cribs* (2002)

35

5. *The Nick Cannon Show* (2002)
6. *Raising Dad* (played "Marvin" in episode: "Bully") (April 26, 2002)
7. *Soul Train* (February 15, 2003)
8. *Romeo!* (series star) (September 13, 2003)

P Miller Shorties
Sportswear for Kids
* velour warm-up sets
* polos
* active wear
* shoes
* jeans

CHAPTER 6

The Girlies

The rap mini master reveals his thoughts on Juliets and Honeys!

"Hey, Romeo, do you have a girlfriend?"

That's what all the little girlies shout out to the pint-sized rapper wherever he goes. When Lil' Romeo blushes and whispers, "Not right now" female Lil' Romeo fans go into overdrive! Technicolor, 3-D romantic daydreams take over. "Maybe *I* could be Lil' Romeo's Juliet?" thousands of girls wonder hopefully!

Actually, Lil' Romeo gives few hints on what would make him sit up and take notice when a little cutie pie crosses his path. When asked about the qualities his dream girl must have, Lil' Romeo reveals, "She should be someone who is nice and likes to have fun, and she should be sort of outgoing."

But then he follows up those remarks with a warning about getting romantically involved at this point in time. "I'm too busy for all that," he explains. "I'm just working on my music. I'm just trying to have a lot of fun. I might, probably in the future."

Don't Give Up!

Even though Lil' Romeo is keeping his attention directly on his professional goals right now, there's no telling who might cross his path and start his heart thumping. Love can take anyone by surprise — anytime, anywhere.

So how do you get Lil' Romeo to notice you? Easy — write the ultimate fan letter to him. That *could* be the best way to his heart.

Here are a few tips on what to put in and what to leave out in your letter to Lil' Romeo.

Dos
- Pick colorful stationery — something bright and cheery like *SpongeBob Squarepants* yellow.
- Use a contrasting color felt-tip pen to write

with. You want your words to POP off the page. Why not try a ruby red?

- First, tell Lil' Romeo why you like him, which of his songs is your personal favorite, and why it is special to you.
- Next, tell him about YOU. Share the things that you like to do. Give him a sample of your favorite school subjects, movies, video games, etc. You might go into a little detail on a subject if you know that you *really* like the same thing he does — like basketball, for example.
- Tell him why you would like to meet him and be his friend.
- Enclose a picture of yourself.
- When you seal the envelope, decorate it with some fun stickers so it might catch his eye.

Don'ts
- Do not write a ten-page letter. Lil' Romeo won't have the time to read a long, long letter. Keep your note short and fun.
- Do not get too sticky and syrupy. Don't gush. Keep your letter interesting and friendly.
- Do not ask unreasonable requests. Remember, Lil' Romeo is not going to be able to come and

visit you for your birthday. And he's not going to buy you a Benz to match the one he has at home! Be realistic — you'll have a better chance of hearing back from him that way.

- Do not get upset if you don't hear back from Lil' Romeo right away.

Okay, you've got all the info you need to write the ultimate Lil' Romeo fan letter. But first, why not take a few minutes to practice in the space below. Use a pencil — you might want to change a word or two.

Dear Lil' Romeo,

_____

_____

_____

_____

_____

_____

_____

_____

_____

_____

_____

_____

_____

_____

_____

_____

_____

_____

_____

_____

_____

_____

_____

_____

_____

_____

_____

_____

Now, get busy! Write your letter, seal it, stamp it,
and send it to:
Nickelodeon
c/o Lil' Romeo
1515 Broadway
New York, NY 10036

CHAPTER 7
Game Time

Now's the time to test your Lil' Romeo knowledge! If you are a true-blue fan, you'll probably know all the answers — most of which are already on the pages of this *Pop People* book. Okay, have some fun, fun, fun!

Fill In the Blanks

1. Which member of Lil' Romeo's family acts as his road manager? _____

2. Which member of Lil' Romeo's family is his role model? _____

3. Which historical figure does Lil' Romeo most admire? _____

4. What is Lil' Romeo's favorite subject in school?

_____

5. What cartoon opened up Lil' Romeo's Spring 2002 tour? _____

Multiple Choice

1. Lil' Romeo admits his worst habit is . . .
   a) biting his nails
   b) playing practical jokes
   c) popping his gum
   d) telling white lies

2. If Lil' Romeo were a wrestler, he would go by . . .
   a) "Golden Child"
   b) "Scoop"
   c) "King Romeo"
   d) "Master Romeo"

3. Lil' Romeo's favorite McDonald's meal is . . .
   a) Big Mac with fries
   b) Chicken Caesar Salad
   c) McGriddles
   d) Egg, Cheese, and Bacon Biscuits

4. The most points Lil' Romeo ever scored in a basketball game was . . .
   a) 120
   b) 42
   c) 18
   d) 60

5. Which of the following names would Lil' Romeo *NOT* answer to?
   a) Romie
   b) Percy
   c) Montaque
   d) Leo

6. The keyboard in Lil' Romeo's studio once belonged to what famous singer/songwriter?
   a) Justin Timberlake
   b) Stevie Wonder
   c) Eminem
   d) Ruben Studdard

7. Which of the following household chores does Lil' Romeo not have to do?
   a) take out the trash
   b) clean his room

Lil' Romeo is the youngest artist to top the *Billboard* charts.

Lil' Romeo chills with his pops Master P—rap's first father and son team. "My dad really inspires me and he guides me."

Lil' Romeo gives props to the crowd.

And never forgets his fans ...
" If I weren't having fun I wouldn't be doing this."

Best advice? "You should do your best in everything ... staying in school and getting good grades is important."

Lil' Romeo and fellow *Honey* co-star Jessica Alba:
"She's like a big sister to me."

Lil' Romeo's got skills. He was named Most Valuable Player in Michael Jordan's summer camp.

Lil' Romeo accepts an award and a hug from his mom. "She is the greatest mom I could have."

With hit albums, movie roles, and a new TV show, the sky's the limit for this pint-sized rapper.

c) drive his brothers and sisters to school
d) feed his dog Dollar

8. Which fast-food restaurant gave away Lil' Romeo's CD single "2 Way" with the purchase of a Mighty Kids Meal?
   a) McDonald's
   b) Wendy's
   c) Taco Bell
   d) Burger King

9. Which female celebrity would Lil' Romeo most like to meet?
   a) Mariah Carey
   b) Hilary Duff
   c) J. Lo
   d) Alicia Keys

10. On school nights Lil' Romeo's curfew is . . .
    a) midnight
    b) 9 or 10 p.m.
    c) 8 p.m.
    d) 11 p.m.

Trivia Treasures

No more guesswork, here are some fascinating facts to impress your Lil' Romeo fan-pals!

1. **The first time Lil' Romeo heard "My Baby" on the radio, he was in Los Angeles.**

    "I heard it on 100.3 THE Beat. I couldn't believe it," recalls Lil' Romeo.

2. **Romeo attended the Michael Jordan basketball camp in Summer 2000.**

    "I was named the camp's Most Valuable Player," Lil' Romeo proudly recalls.

3. **When Lil' Romeo was a little shorty, Shaquille O'Neal lived near his house and used to come over to shoot some hoops with Master P. Lil' Romeo would sometimes join them and Shaq would pick him up to make a basket.**

    "When I looked up at him, I got dizzy!" Lil' Romeo laughs.

4. **Master P and Lil' Romeo will never forget where they came from — the Calliope projects in New Orleans, Louisiana. When**

they appeared on CBS's *48 Hours Investigates* in June 2003, they even visited their old apartment.

"3649 Eradi Street, Apartment B."

5. Lil' Romeo will never forget the first time he performed on TV.

"It was on MTV with my dad [on his song] "'Bout Dat,'" says Lil' Romeo.

6. Lil' Romeo describes his style of rapping.

"I rap like my dad. I rap any way. I rap East Coast, West Coast, and the South. So everybody can listen to my music."

7. *Romeo!* was not the original name of Lil' Romeo's TV series on Nickelodeon.

"Originally, the show was called *Pieces of the Puzzle*," says Lil' Romeo.

8. Lil' Romeo claims his music has helped him in his acting, too.

"I like to listen to music while I'm learning my lines," he says. "It's kind of like hearing somebody rap, and it just sticks to my brain."

47

Answers

Fill In the Blanks

1. His mom, Sonja
2. His dad, Master P
3. Martin Luther King, Jr.
4. Math — "I love math. If they didn't have math, I wouldn't want to go to school!" Lil' Romeo told a reporter.
5. Warner Brothers' *Merrie Melodies*.

Multiple Choice

1. c — popping his gum
2. a — "Golden Child"
3. d — Egg, Cheese, and Bacon Biscuits
4. b — 42
5. c — Montaque. Romie is one of his nicknames, Percy is his real first name, and Leo is his secret nickname.
6. b — Stevie Wonder
7. c — drive his brothers and sisters to school — Lil' Romeo doesn't have his driver's license yet!
8. a — McDonald's
9. c — "J. Lo — who else?" Lil' Romeo told *Nickelodeon* magazine.
10. b — 9 or 10 p.m.

CHAPTER 8

Did'ja Know?

If you are a fan of Lil' Romeo's, these are must-know facts!

Did'ja Know... Lil' Romeo is on the advisory committee for Nickelodeon's Let's Just Play campaign? This program encourages kids to be active and involved in sports, school, and community activities.

Did'ja Know... Lil' Romeo dedicated the song "We Can Make It Right" from his *Game Time* album to all the people who lost their lives on September 11, 2001, at the World Trade Center? He wanted to share his feelings with the victims' families and friends.

Did'ja Know... The only people who call Lil'

Romeo by his given name, Percy, are his grandparents?

Did'ja Know . . . Lil' Romeo not only loves math, but English, too? "I love learning about verbs, adjectives, and nouns, and where to put commas and stuff like that. It's cool."

Did'ja Know . . . Someone posed as a No Limit representative and took orders for Lil' Romeo concert tickets, CDs, and clothes from Chicago students? When Master P and Lil' Romeo found out about the scam, they went to Chicago and appeared at North Side High School. They invited students from the five schools who had been cheated. They gave a pep talk and encouraged them to stay in school and work hard at achieving their goals — and local rap station WPWX gave the students back the money they had spent on the bogus items. Then Master P asked everyone to join him on the school's basketball court where he played a game of one-on-one with the head of the Chicago public schools!

Did'ja Know . . . in Lil' Romeo's Houston, Texas, house he has brightly colored chairs shaped like big hands? You sit in the "palm" and the "fingers" are the back of the chair. "They are everybody's favorite chairs," says Lil' Romeo.

Did'ja Know . . . that a magazine once stated that

Lil' Romeo hated spinach? It was wrong! "I like vegetables and fruits, anything that can make me healthy," Lil' Romeo corrected the mistake.

Did'ja Know . . . Lil' Romeo and his brother Vercy always play NBA Courtside on their GameCube video game player? "I always win," insists Lil' Romeo.

Did'ja Know . . . Lil' Romeo is a "tasty" cover boy? Right — he's on the package of Rap Snacks Barbecue Chips and Honey Chips. Mmmm!

Did'ja Know . . . Lil' Romeo is a fan of books by Matt Christopher, the author of *Johnny Long Legs*? "I read all his books," says the straight-A rapper. "He writes about sports. He's a good author. I read his books, like, in one day."

Did'ja Know . . . Lil' Romeo and his brothers and sisters go to church every Sunday? Master P and Sonja Miller made that a family rule.

Did'ja Know . . . Lil' Romeo's uncle, rapper Silkk the Shocker, says his nephew is just like his dad, Master P? "They're exactly alike," says Silkk.

Did'ja Know . . . Lil' Romeo actually met his longtime idol, Michael Jackson? "I was really excited. I performed at his anniversary party. It was kind of weird meeting someone that you really look up to."

CHAPTER 9

Lil' Romeo Reveals All from the Heart

Listen up . . . he has a lot to say!

Chip Off the Block

* The best thing about having a famous dad like Master P is . . . "going on the road, watching my dad do his concerts, and just seeing him do his thing. I get to have a lot of fun with my dad, traveling and looking over the business."

* My dad really supports everything I do . . . "He encouraged me to be a rapper. I probably wouldn't be a rapper if he wasn't a rapper. It's a tough job for a kid."

* The person I admire the most is . . . "my dad, because he's the best basketball player I know."

* I listen to my dad because . . . "he's been in the

business for ten years, so it's a real help to have him on the road. He'll always give me tips and advice and stuff."

* The best advice my dad has given me is . . . "You gotta work hard and always practice what you do." And "Stay on rhythm!"

Mama's Little Boy

* I helped write "Little Star" from *Lil' Romeo* . . . "It's about my mom, 'cause she is the greatest mom I could have."

Family Ties

* Master P says Lil' Romeo is naturally responsible . . . "When he's on the road, he's constantly buying stuff for his brother and sisters. When I ain't around, he knows he needs to step up and take care of the family."

* The thing I value most is . . . "my family. I'm doing this for them."

Friendship

* My regular friends knew me before . . . "I was a rapper, but when I started making my songs, they were like, 'I heard your song on the radio and it's weird 'cause I knew you before you was a rapper.' It felt weird to them because they were sitting right next to me and I was making songs. But I have regular friends and I'm a regular kid."

Scary Thoughts
* **My greatest fear is . . .** "never playing basketball again and not being able to make records."

Twinkle, Twinkle, Lil' Star
* **Being a child star is tough because . . .** "not everybody believes in you or thinks you can do a lot of stuff, 'cause you're a kid. It's hard being away from my family, going on tour, but it's also a lot of good time. It feels good to know the fans really care."

A Devastating Loss
* **The saddest time in my life was . . .** "when my cousin, Lance, was fifteen years old, he was in a Jeep and I was in the car with him. I was about eight or nine. He was in the passenger seat. The Jeep flipped over three times. Lance and I used to do music with each other. [There were three other people in the car] — me, a five-year-old, and an eighteen-year-old. Lance was the only one that died.

Nobody else got hurt or injured. I dedicated a song to him on my first album, because me and him used to always play basketball and music."

Witnessing History
* I will never forget September 11, 2001, because . . . "we were supposed to be, like, two blocks away [from the World Trade Center]. But my dad didn't want to wake me up, because I overslept. My mom was, like, 'Go wake up Romeo,' but he said, 'No, let him sleep.' So we were late and I slept. So we didn't go. . . . When the first plane hit we thought it was an accident, and then when the second plane hit, we figured out it was a terrorist attack. But then we noticed that we were supposed to be two blocks away from there and we were like, 'Oh, this is crazy.' And we were real thankful that we didn't go, real blessed."

Lil' Romeo and his family were supposed to head back to Los Angeles after that, but instead of flying they hit the road in their tour bus. "We drove — it took us six days to get back to where we were going to," says Lil' Romeo. "We had to go to Los Angeles, because that's where my brothers and sisters were. We had to go all the way down there, but we had to go to Atlanta first, then we had to fly in an airplane to Los Angeles. And that took us about seven hours, the planes were all delayed."

Lil' Romeo Makes A Wish
* We love the Make A Wish Foundation . . . "My dad and me, we [are] always there for all of the kids," explains the thirteen-year-old rapper. "Every Thanksgiving and every Christmas — we'll give the Make A Wish Foundation some toys, like Game-Boys for Christmas, and for Thanksgiving we'll give them turkeys. We gave over ten thousand turkeys [last] year for Thanksgiving, and two thousand GameBoys and GameCubes for Christmas. I also have the Lil' Romeo Foundation, which gives back to the communities and the less fortunate."

A Laugh A Minute
* One of my favorite jokes is . . . "A turtle walks into the grocery store and asks the clerk, 'Do you have grapes?' The clerk says, 'No.' The next day, the turtle is back again and he says, 'Do you have any grapes?' 'No, I don't sell grapes,' says the clerk. This goes on all week. So, the angry clerk finally says, 'If you ask for grapes one more time, I'm going to staple your feet to the floor!' The next day, the turtle

comes back and says, 'Do you have any staples?' The clerk says, 'No.' 'Okay, then do you have grapes?' the turtle asks."

Smiley Face
* **The thing I like best is . . .** "seeing the fans happy and smiling."

Up Close and Personal
* **I want all my fans to know . . .** "that I'm just a laid-back, regular kid."

Advice
* **I will always believe this . . .** "like Martin Luther King, Jr., said, have a dream, have a dream."

An Inquiring Mind
* **To get ahead in school . . .** "always pay attention and always study that subject real hard. Study, go over it three times, and then you'll see the next day how good you did or not. If you can't study that good, you might need to get a tutor, if you need help. . . . Never be afraid to ask for help. I always ask a lot of questions in school."

CHAPTER 10
Beat Street

**"I make music for the kids because I'm young —
that's why I came out to make music with clean
lyrics for the kids, positive music to teach them.
I think that's a real important thing."**

— Lil' Romeo

Back in 2001, no one expected an eleven-year-old
talent to erupt out of the No Limit Records family.
No one, that is, except the founder and CEO of No
Limit, Master P — and that high-voltage talent
was his oldest son, Lil' Romeo.

When eleven-year-old Lil' Romeo's first single,
"My Baby," was heard over the radio airwaves, it
became clear that the fresh-faced, newest member
of the Lil' club had a hit on his hands. One news reporter wrote in an article that when "My Baby" became number one on both *Billboard*'s Pop and Rap/

R&B charts, the P in Master P's name could stand for "Proud Papa" or "Publicist."

Proud papa or publicist — whatever! Master P was glad to have Lil' Romeo take the stage, front and center. "This is just the beginning for history-making with this project," Master P told MTV News at the time. "When Romeo's album is released, I believe we will also [become] the first father-and-son MC's to have achieved platinum status with our solo projects. . . . This is something bigger than me. We made sure his music is for kids and the beats are something the adults could grab on to. Lil' Romeo is gonna take No Limit to the next level."

Master P was right! And Lil' Romeo understood he was making his mark in hip-hop history. "I think I'm opening the doors a lot," the future mini mogul told MTV during an interview. "Like Another Bad Creation did, like Lil' Bow Wow. All the kids open up the doors. They opened it for me and we'll open it for other kids and do this thing right."

The Write Stuff

Lil' Romeo has actually been writing his own rhymes since he was six years old. Of course, he had a master teacher in Master P. Lil' Romeo along with his dad has co-written many of the songs on both his albums, *Lil' Romeo* and *Game Time*.

And how does Lil' Romeo come up with his lyrics? Well, first there's the beat. He starts with "whatever I like to listen to and what I think kids like to listen to."

"I know it's a hot track when my cousins like it and start bouncing to the music," says Lil' Romeo. "If nobody bounces to the music, it's not a beat for me. . . . Then the lyrics flow after that."

The next step is to run it by his dad. "It's just a lot of fun to know that I have writing skills to write my own album," says Lil' Romeo. "And my dad writes with me, so me and him go back and forth writing and making hits."

"I kind of oversee Romeo when he writes to make sure he's going in the right direction," says Master P of the magical father-son writing process.

And the "right direction" means dealing with kid-friendly topics. "I just try to help all the kids out there," explains Lil' Romeo of his raps. "Like, let them know that education always comes first, always listen to your parents, and stuff like that — teach them that in the songs. I always give them something to believe in and [tell them to] always have a lot of fun in [their] life. On my *Lil' Romeo* album I had the ABC song, and everybody liked that song. We perform that sometimes and get a big response — it teaches the young kids how to do their ABC's."

But this lifestyle teaches Lil' Romeo a life lesson, too. His dad will only allow him to continue performing as long as he keeps his grades on the A and B level, and only as long as he's having fun. Right now it's all good — Lil' Romeo is an honor student and he happily tells anyone who will listen, "I get tired, and it can be hard, but it's so fun . . . being in the studio is so fun!"

Spotlight on the Songs in Lil' Romeo's Heart
Favorite Master P Songs:
* "Make 'Em Say Uh" and "To My Hommies Passed Away," an R&B song.
All-Time Favorite Song:
* Michael Jackson's "I'll Be There."
"My Baby" from his Lil' Romeo album:
* "My favorite song is probably 'My Baby' — it was number one for ten weeks."
* "My Baby" samples the beat of the Jackson Five's "I Want You Back." "It was a real good pop song," Lil'

Romeo explains. "I liked the Jackson 5 a long time ago. I used to listen to that song and I really liked it. We made a deal and I got that track behind it."
* The "My Baby" video features Lil' Romeo on the basketball court — and hanging out with a Michael Jackson look-alike.

Game Time Tidbits
* Originally, *Game Time* was due out in Summer 2002, but was released in December 2002. "I wanted to do a few more songs," Lil' Romeo explains of the delay. "I thought that it was better to make it as a Christmas album. This is my second album. I thought it would be a good stocking stuffer. We used that [extra] time and made it into a bigger record. [We added] the single with Solange ['True Love'] and 'Feel Like Dancing.' It's a party song, a real fun song for the girls to dance to."
* Lil' Romeo wrote or cowrote 16 of the 19 songs on his *Game Time* album.
* "2 Way" was the first single from *Game Time*.
* "I sampled a little bit more on this album," Lil' Romeo says of *Game Time*. "I like sampling because a lot of kids don't get to hear the music from way back, so I bring it so they can hear it."

* "2 Way" sampled bits from Rob Base and DJ E-Z Rock's "It Takes Two."

* The video for "2 Way" took three days to shoot. In the video, Lil' Romeo has a b-ball court battle with . . . himself! "I have an evil and a good me!" Romeo laughs. "We have a big 'ol basketball game." During the shoot, Lil' Romeo was attached to wires so they could have him dunking the ball from the free throw line like a mini Michael Jordan.

* Nick Quested, the director of "2 Way," was impressed with Lil' Romeo's court ability. "Romeo plays himself at the basketball [game] and he makes the most incredible shots. Romeo's already got game. The whole family's obsessed with basketball. All they need is a hoop and ball."

* "True Love" — the single he did with Solange — was the second single from *Game Time*. Lil' Romeo had a blast working with Solange, the little sister of Destiny's Child's Beyoncé. "It was a lot of fun," says Lil' Romeo. "[Solange] is from the same hometown as me, H-town — Houston, Texas. All the fans — I wanna thank them for making the video [a success]."

CHAPTER 11
Welcome to Lil' Romeo's Home Court

If Lil' Romeo inherited his love of music and hip-hop from his dad, well, Master P passed on something else, too — the love of basketball! Standing 6 feet 4 inches tall, Master P once dreamed of being an NBA star. Though he put it on the back burner when he started up No Limit Records, Master P never lost his desire to play with the big boys of the NBA. Even while he was running the multi-million dollar business of No Limit, Master P took time off to try out for some professional basketball teams. He got signed for a brief time to the Toronto Raptors and the Charlotte Hornets. And when Michael Jordan took over the Washington Wizards, Master P followed for another tryout. Unfortunately, he never made a team for a full season, but that didn't stop him from loving basketball!

Romeo's Court Skills

Lil' Romeo has been playing basketball since he could walk. He and his dad shoot one-on-one hoops almost every day they are together. Even when they are working on the set of *Romeo!*, they have a half-court just off the set so they can work off their excess energy.

When Lil' Romeo isn't working or studying, he's perfecting his basketball skills. He plays point guard on the AAU team called the No Limit Ballers. And guess who's the coach? Master P, of course!

Lil' Romeo has made a name for himself in this youth league. In 2002 he was ranked number one in the 12-year-olds' division, and his team was ranked number two out of 98 teams across the country. Lil' Romeo has attended the Michael Jordan summer basketball camp for several years, and in 2002 he was named camp MVP!

"My dream has always been to be an NBA player," says Lil' Romeo. "My dad really inspired me and he guides me a lot. I have seen him in the NBA and it was fun watching him. I want people to watch me and have a good game."

CHAPTER 12

Lil' Romeo Screen Time: Lights . . . Camera . . . Action!

Rapping on stage or on TV for millions of fans is not the only arena Lil' Romeo has conquered. He's been bitten by the acting bug ever since he appeared in a small role in the feature film *Max Keeble's Big Move*.

Well, Lil' Romeo's made a few big moves of his own since then. Though music is still his first love, he put off going into the studio to work on his third album in 2003 in order to get in front of the cameras.

"Acting has always been one of my hobbies," says Lil' Romeo. "Me and my cousin used to have a little camcorder to record stuff, so I'm real excited."

How Lil' Romeo Became *Romeo!*
Shortly after Lil' Romeo released his debut album, he and his dad established a relationship with the

hot kids' TV network, Nickelodeon. Master P and Nickelodeon discussed establishing a relationship with Lil' Romeo — series, specials, spokesman, all that and more.

"I did a couple of voice-overs for Nick, and I guess they liked what I was doing, so we shot a pilot and everybody liked it," Lil' Romeo recalls. That was the pilot for his series *Romeo!* — originally called *Pieces of the Puzzle*.

"I'm really excited about my new sitcom, *Romeo!*, on Nickelodeon," Lil' Romeo told reporters. "It's my dad and me doing a modern-day *Partridge Family* type of thing. Since I had a small role in *Max Keeble's Big Move*, and did some television with *The Hughleys* and *Raising Dad*, I felt really comfortable in front of the cameras again. Plus, working with my dad is great. He's been in the business for many years, so I feel honored to have him by my side. He knows the rights and wrongs and the dos and don'ts."

It would seem natural for Lil' Romeo to feel at ease with *Romeo!*, since there are so many similarities between the plot of the show and his own life. Of course, there are a few more obstacles for the reel-life Romeo to overcome than the real-life Romeo.

"My character, he's hungry, he wants to be successful and he wants to be number one," explains Lil' Romeo of his on-screen alter ego. "That's why he's always sneaking into radio stations and making plans to perform at his high school. . . . This show is about a family coming together through music and a lot of people can relate to that because a lot of families get together through music. This show's about a real comedy and it touches a lot of kid issues."

Not only is Master P one of the stars of *Romeo!*, he's also the producer. He wanted to make sure that while there were lots of laughs in the sitcom, a message was included, too. "In the show, I'm the one [who] makes sure we put all the pieces to the puzzle [together]," he explains. "Like Romeo said, [there's] a lot of comedy and a lot of family issues in the show as well. I think the thing that makes the show different is me and Romeo being the first hip-hop father and son to get together. . . . We're definitely breaking down a lot of barriers. I think we're going to be successful in this and it's going to enable us to go after bigger opportunities. And I feel this is going to inspire kids to go after bigger [goals] themselves. It's gonna show kids that they don't have to sit around and be hard all day. This is for real, you can be yourself and go after other avenues of being successful. You can choose your dreams and goals."

Official *Romeo!* Q&A

During a Nickelodeon press conference right before *Romeo!* debuted, Master P and Lil' Romeo fielded questions about the show. You're invited to sneak a peek.

Q: Master P — you guys [New No Limit artists] are not quite the Nickelodeon audience. . . .
Master P: Well, you know, I think that's the great thing about this — to be able to come from somewhere else. And that's what I like about the Nickelodeon family, you know, [they were] able to let us come from a different world, and say, "We're all a part of the family," to tell that television is changing, music is changing, the world is changing.

Q: Lil' Romeo — how do you see *Romeo!* working into your life?
Lil' Romeo: Well, I think this show will be a good thing for me, 'cause it'll break me out to different things, like bigger roles in movies and other things like that.

Q: Master P, what's it like working with your son?

Master P: It's definitely a blessing, you know, to be able to work with your child. And most times you be far away, and now it's, like, we're there together. We're almost friends now, you know, we're like buddies. . . . It makes you feel good that we're growing up together — we're going through different experiences together. . . . We wanted to show people that we're talented, and we could go to any direction. I think Romeo is one of the next greatest child stars, as far as acting. I mean, I consider him a modern-day Will Smith.

Q: Lil' Romeo, what's it like working with your dad?

Lil' Romeo: Well, it's just a lot of fun . . . and it's just a great thing because, usually, like, when you have child actors, they're far away from their parents.

Get the scoop on Lil' Romeo's upcoming movie projects:

Honey
Stars: Lil' Romeo, Jessica Alba, Mekhi Phifer
Movie Company: Universal

Release Date: November 14, 2003

Plot: Jessica Alba is Honey Daniels, a dancer/choreographer who pays the rent by working as a bartender and record store clerk. She's just waiting for her big break. When that break comes, Honey realizes that there are other dreams, too — one of which is helping a group of talented neighborhood kids, led by Benny (Lil' Romeo), make their own mark on the dance floor. Benny comes from a broken home and faces the temptations of easy money. But Honey sweeps in and takes Benny under her wing and shows him the best way to focus all his energies . . . by dancing.

All about *Honey*

"It was a lot of fun working with Jessica," admits Lil' Romeo. "She's like a big sister to me. She told me what to do, but in a fun way. We always had little mini play fights. She was messing with me. It was real cool. My character's name is Benny. He's from the 'hood; he's trying to make it out."

But working on *Honey* wasn't all fun and games and goofing off with Jessica. There was plenty of hard work, too. "We had to do two months of dance rehearsals and three months of shooting," recalls Lil' Romeo. "My videos [take] only three days [to shoot]. It's a big difference. It takes patience. At first I was frustrated because I wasn't used to dancing. I wasn't really trying to do it, but then, after finding out people really liked it, it made me like it better. It was a lot of fun."

Shorty

"It's kind of like *E.T.*," reveals Lil' Romeo. "I become friends with an alien that lands on Earth. We have things in common — we both like music. I teach him how to rap by performing some of my old songs, and he learns English from me. . . . I learn from him and he learns from me, so it's going to be a real good movie. And my dad is going to be a bad guy in this movie. It's a real tight movie."

Shorty is currently awaiting a release date.

Uncle P

Once again, Master P hooks up with Lil' Romeo in front of the movie cameras. This time, in *Uncle P*, he plays a millionaire hip-hop entrepreneur who drops out of the dog-eat-dog world of business so he can help out his sister's family. She is ill and can't take care of her three kids, so Uncle P arrives on the scene. The suburbs of California are totally alien to Uncle P. What does he know about mowing lawns and walking a dog? He's an inner-city guy.

CHAPTER 13
All That Glitters

Okay, we've mentioned that Lil' Romeo's dad is an extremely successful businessman. Master P is the head of his own record company, he's a movie and TV producer, artist manager, and he owns a clothing company. According to CBS's *48 Hours Investigates*, Master P is worth over $400 million! That's right — $400 million!

The Millers own fabulous homes in Houston, Baton Rouge, and Los Angeles. They stay at beautiful hotel suites and have traveled all over the world. They have a stretch limousine with a fireplace in it and big old bodyguards who travel everywhere with Lil' Romeo. And, of course, you can't forget Lil' Romeo's customized Mercedes Benz and Hummer that sit in his garage!

All That Glitters Is Not Gold

With all this bling-bling, you might think that Lil' Romeo could be just another spoiled little rich kid. But that's not the case at all! Lil' Romeo remembers where his family came from — the hard streets of the projects. He knows how hard his father and his mother had to work to create such a wonderful life for their family. Indeed, when asked what he values most in his life, Lil' Romeo forgets all about the Mercedes, the diamond pendants, and the superstar lifestyle. Instead, he says with all his heart, "My family, I have to say. Family always gonna be there. The material things, they come and go."

Now, statements like that make a papa proud. "It's just a blessing to see that he's so levelheaded," says Master P. "You know, because he's such a big star. I mean, I [see] girls chasing him everywhere he goes. . . . But I'm always teaching him that the way you gonna build the muscles in your brain, you gotta read. . . . I never expected Romeo to grow up and be a big superstar entertainer. I was just like, 'Man, this is my child. I want him to have better things than me.'"

Well, Master P has definitely made that dream come true!

CHAPTER 14

Stay Tuned for More Lil' Romeo . . .

"My dad always thought big, but I used to think, 'Is everybody gonna like me?' and I wondered if I was gonna do well," Lil' Romeo recalls of his early days, when he first released his debut album.

With the success of his albums, movies, and TV show, Lil' Romeo has stopped wondering if anyone was ever going to like him! Instead, he wants to thank each and every one of his fans who have supported him and brought him to where he is now. "Right now, all the fans are being loyal to me and like me and I really appreciate that," he says. "I'm real happy. It's just a blessing to accomplish your dream."

Actually, Lil' Romeo hopes the fact that he's attained so many of his goals helps other kids realize they can, too. Maybe they won't be hip-hop superstars or NBA players, but they can work hard, study hard, and become doctors, lawyers, teachers, anything they really want. And there's another thing — Lil' Romeo wants to let his fans know that they should *never* stop dreaming. Even though he's reached the heights of fame and fortune, there are plenty more things he wants to do. And one of them is to get a good education. He even told one reporter that he might take a little break from show business real soon.

"I'm doing everything I want to do," he said. "I'm doing it right now. But [soon] I'll probably just go to school for a while, just go to high school."

Don't worry! Even if Lil' Romeo does decide to be a kid for a while, he'll never give up the stage. He'll be back . . . and you can bet, better than ever before!